Mystical Prayer Is for (Almost) Everyone

Ernest J. Fiedler

FOREWORD BY
Lawrence S. Cunningham

Paulist Press
New York/Mahwah, NJ

Cover design by Sharyn Banks
Cover photo credit: Anton de Flon
Book design by Lynn Else

Library of Congress Cataloging-in-Publication Data

Fiedler, Ernest J.
    Mystical prayer is for (almost) everyone / Ernest J. Fiedler ; foreword by Lawrence S. Cunningham.
        p. cm.
    Includes bibliographical references (p.   ).
    ISBN 978-0-8091-4576-8 (alk. paper)
    1. Contemplation. 2. Prayer—Catholic Church. 3. Mysticism—Catholic Church. I. Title. II. Title: Mystical prayer is for everyone.
    BV5091.C7.F543 2009
    248.3—dc22

                                                    2008047572

Published by Paulist Press
997 Macarthur Boulevard
Mahwah, New Jersey 07430

www.paulistpress.com

Printed and bound in the
United States of America

Contents

THE GOAL OF THIS BOOK...

The Constitution on the Sacred Liturgy, the first document of the Second Vatican Council, teaches that the liturgy is the "summit and source" of our prayer (§10). This small book recognizes and heartily embraces that truth and hopes to assist its realization by assisting deeper private and personal prayer to the end called for in that document.

Foreword

$\mathcal{O}$ ne of the more enjoyable aspects of being on the theology faculty at the University of Notre Dame is the opportunity to teach in the summer program there and at the other schools that invite some of us to join their summer faculty. Over the past two decades I have enjoyed the hospitality of Spring Hill College in Mobile, Alabama; Saint John's in Collegeville, Minnesota; Saint Elizabeth's College in Convent Station, New Jersey; and Boston College in Chestnut Hill, Massachusetts. But always, either before or after those travels, I have taught in the summer program at Notre Dame.

I describe all those experiences as enjoyable for the simple reason that the summer semester, unlike the regular term, affords me the chance to interact with older students, many of whom have a long experience in the pastoral life of the church. Summer courses attract lay persons involved in continuing education; priests and religious who use the opportunity to combine schooling with summer vacation; high school teachers who come to update their certification; and lots of people, from every walk of life, who simply want to deepen their knowledge of the faith. What they all bring to the class is a world of experience and a hunger for learning of a type quite different from the undergraduates whom we meet during the year. It is frequently the case that I have learned from my summer students as much as I have taught.

Among the many wonderful people I met on the campus of Notre Dame over the years was Monsignor Ernest Fiedler, who was a "regular" with us. Bud (as everyone called him) took classes and was at the center of bull sessions in the lunchroom and a frequent, and most welcome, visitor during office hours. It was a terrible shock to learn that he had died before Christmas in 2007 after he had submitted the manuscript for this present book. He had been a student of mine and of Professor Bernard McGinn, who taught for us in the summer. In fact, it was Dr. McGinn, the preeminent historian of Christian mysticism, who sent me a message about Bud's death.

Bud came to my office a few summers ago to tell me of his idea of writing a little book for lay people on the subject of deep prayer and asked me what I thought about the notion. I not only encouraged him to begin to write, but also volunteered to read a draft of anything he wrote and to help him find a venue for its publication. We kept in regular contact over the phone. When he sent me his first draft, I urged him to make it a little longer (not always advice I give to many who seem to write a lot and to say little!), but I remember telling him that he had struck the right tone and had a gift for prose that was both crisp and direct. Alas, he died before he had a chance to see this book between covers; with its publication, it is his final act of ministry.

There are many things that made Bud such a wonderful person. He was a deeply committed priest who loved his ministry and those to whom he ministered. Even in retirement he had an insatiable desire to learn and an equal zeal to teach others. Profoundly Catholic, he was not one of those hand wringers who thought everything was going to hell in a hand basket. Most of all, it was clear that he was a priest who had been deeply formed after his decades of service to the people of God. The only way I was able to detect the depths of Bud's spiritual life was through his desire to communicate the life of deep prayer to others. Sometimes the superficially spiritual try to write on prayer but what they write rings hollow; readers of this work will soon find out that what Bud wrote rings true.

I hope no reader will be frightened off by the word *mystical* in the title. Bud knew well that mysticism, mystic, and mystical prayer only mean that which is not evident at first glance. The fathers used the adjective *mystical* to describe the Eucharist, the scriptures, and the Church. At first glance those realities meant bread, a book, and an organization.

Seen through the eyes of faith, those same realities meant the Real Presence, the Word of God, and the body of Christ. When Bud speaks of mystical prayer, he is speaking of the One who stands behind the words we utter. He wants us to find the Mystery behind the quotidian. To speak of such matters correctly, we should know what we are talking about at a personal level. Bud learned from two sources: the books of the tradition as well as what the great mystic St. Bernard of Clairvaux called the "book of experience." It is a mark of Bud's generous spirit that he wished to share that knowledge with others. This little book is a fitting final tribute to the memory of a good priest who is now in a place where the hidden is made radiantly clear.

Lawrence S. Cunningham
John A. O'Brien Professor of Theology
Ordinary Time, 2008

How to...

*T*his is a book for those who already pray and who wish to pray more deeply.

The following segments have a certain loose logical progression but also may be taken individually out of sequence. The goal is to provide a kind of primer of elements to open or assist individual mystical prayer. It is recommended, however, that the first ten segments be studied and prayed first.

Why "For Almost *Everyone*"?

*F*irst of all, because this book is obviously not for someone who does not want to pray or pray more deeply. Also, because the practice of mystical prayer has often been burdened with an unfair assumption that it is an area of prayer intended for a few very special, unusual, and chosen people. This book wishes to present a challenge to that assumption. It is for anyone who sincerely wants to pray better.

It has also been assumed that mystical prayer is so difficult, even exotic, that few people were considered truly able to achieve it. This developed further into the assumption that mystical prayer is usually for "professional" religious people: holy scholars, people already well marked for sanctity of life and religious living in convents and monasteries. This promotes a mistaken opinion that is a part of the challenge of this book. Notice that the laity has not been mentioned. This book is addressed in a special way to them—but not exclusively to them. It is addressed to anyone who has ever experienced an interest or a desire to relate to God more immediately, but does not have the slightest idea whether that is possible and, if it is, how it would be done. This book is for anyone who is sincerely interested in deeper prayer but feels almost totally alone in following up on such an impulse or desire.

How did we come to these assumptions? Leaving aside for a moment persons noted in the Old Testament who seem to be mystical, and leaving aside for a moment the possibility that even some of the ancient Greeks give apparent evidence of a sense of mysticism, what specific evidence do we find in Christian history?

I remember that early in my pursuit of this subject I enrolled in a summer graduate course on St. Anthony of Egypt in order to look for the presence of "the ordinary lay Christian" in that early age of developing spirituality. Anthony is often called the "first hermit" or "founder of monasticism." I was anxious to learn whether the laity was mentioned at that time (Anthony lived between 251 and 356). The only mention of the laity was the assumption that laypeople were among those who called Anthony out of his hermitage more than once to guide them or assist in the struggle with Arianism, the first widespread heresy in the Church. When some of these people went to follow his then-chosen lifestyle, this was considered to be the beginning of monasticism. Nonetheless, the presence of the laity in historical accounts of the period was peripheral.

St. Athanasius, a contemporary and major voice against the Arian heresy, wrote about the life of Anthony around 357—the first "life-of-a-saint" account. But he does not let his attention wander far from the main character of his "life," Anthony himself, and does not address the prayer of the laity in that early period.

From late antiquity into the early Middle Ages certain directions were set. The laity was increasingly illiterate and the clergy was the educated class of society. This obviously had a strong effect on recorded history and any in-depth study of prayer by the laity. As one pursues history from that point on, these factors become dominant.

When the scholars and students of divine revelation in scripture increasingly investigated the hidden but unfolding mysteries of the Christian faith, they began to note its prayer life and some possible mystical experiences. But evidence for a specific investigation of mystical prayer for and from the laity is slim indeed, even though the letters of the New Testament, especially those of St. Paul and St. John, are obviously addressed to the "ordinary believer" or those who might become believers. Many of the later scholars are remembered today because their writings were often conserved in the form of written sermons and homilies. Who were the audiences of these homilies? Most frequently, because the homilist was a monk, the audience was monastic. Not always, however. As time went on it became evident that these homilies were delivered to larger audiences; however, the recorded practitioners were the specialized few without any significant record of the reactions of the masses, the ordinary lay man or woman.

This historical distancing not only influenced the laity, it also affected the training of the clergy. As recently as during the last fifty years, seminarians were frequently discouraged from reading the mystics on the grounds that it would confuse or misdirect a developing prayer life of students for the priesthood. Again, this reflected the attitude that mystical prayer was only for special people—saints, ascetics, people out of the ordinary way of life—even though the New Testament is addressed to every believing or potential Christian. This book maintains that that is an unfortunate and erroneous point of view, and hopes to rectify it.

Therefore we say "for almost everyone" because the great treasure of mystical prayer should be available to everyone who chooses to explore it.

Do not rush through these pages. The segments are all bite size. Chew and digest them thoughtfully. Periodically there will be pauses called "Practice" written in at the end of certain segments to help you incorporate this material into your own prayer life.

Beginning

In beginning to pray, the first step is to stop. Simply stop. Sit down. Be aware that you are in the presence of God, even if it is an act of faith based on simple intelligence. If God is everywhere, God is here, in this room, in this space, in me. Be comfortable but sit upright.

This awareness may give a momentary sensation of God as a living presence, making himself consciously present to me, at this moment, in my will, in my understanding, perhaps even in my experience, my feeling. It may be very elusive, but I may have just *felt* the living presence of the eternal God. That already is a mystical experience. Mystical prayer is the actual experience of God's presence. Feeling God. Being conscious of God's presence.

Karl Rahner once said he believed that we all have "mystical moments." Sometimes they are quite perceptible for at least a moment, but they do not last. One's mind is constantly deluged with innumerable distractions. The question then becomes: What does one do to keep the connection alive and functioning, and to grow in it? Several things are possible, and these are discussed herein. They are merely aids that can sustain and deepen the consciousness and sense of God's presence that is the heart of contemplative or mystical prayer.

The Mantra

$\mathcal{M}$any people have heard of an old Russian formula called the "Jesus Prayer," or perhaps they have tried "centering prayer," or simply learned to use their own mantra—a word or very short phrase that is repeated over and over, quietly and calmly. These are all ways to begin as well as to continue or refocus on (when distractions take over) the sense of God's presence. It is a very simple but very important tool. Here is how to do it.

Find the quietest place you can, sit comfortably, gently close your eyes or rest them on a simple stationary object that does not demand attention, and be aware that God is everywhere. Begin to repeat a mantra that you have chosen. It can be any word or phrase, but the shorter the better. Something like "Jesus Lord" or "Come, Lord Jesus" is fine, or it can be as simple as "Jesus" as you breathe in, breath out. Gently begin to repeat your mantra either audibly or silently. Soon you will forget the words and find you are simply using them to keep you in contact with the presence of God or Christ.

Let your mind and even your body rest in an awareness of Christ's presence. It may be an intellectual awareness of presence even in "cold, unfeeling" faith or an experience of a brief but elusive, faintly sensible presence. For some moments you may "feel" this presence. The experience is rarely a lasting experience. (Is this not possibly one of Rahner's mystical moments?) When your mind wanders, gently repeat the mantra to refocus on God's presence. Begin with just a few moments. But soon try to set aside ten or fifteen minutes each morning and evening to grow in the perceived serenity of the living presence of God.

PRACTICE: Stop for a few minutes. Decide on a mantra. You may even wish to ask Jesus to help you find a suitable mantra. You can change it later if you wish, but choose one now.

God/Christ

We should pause here to explain the use of the names of *God* and *Christ* in this book. Mystical prayer is about a way of being perceptibly with God—a kind of enveloping thought. In faith we believe that God has become much more immediately present to us by becoming human in Christ. We call that the mystery of the incarnation. The Word remains truly God and becomes also truly human. Because of that, Christ is obviously the most immediate possible connection with God. He is of God's inmost being, in his eternal, supremely mysterious life as Trinity— Father, Son (or Word), and Holy Spirit. So sometimes you will be aware only of being in the presence of wonder. This can be either an experience of the vast otherness (yet presence) of God directly or of God as experienced in Christ. It can even be seen as participation in the way Christ himself experiences the Trinity. Either is correct.

Just think of that! You can be praying the prayer of Christ with Christ. In prayer, then, sometimes you would use "Christ" when the emphasis seems more concrete, and at other times "God" when the encounter seems more indefinable, more elusive. Different people will have different points of awareness or emphasis. ("Jesus" always refers to the historical person.) With that in mind we will often use the name of Christ rather than both names unless the context of our thought demands both names or one or the other of them. Sometimes we will use both in the form "God/Christ." This is possible for the Christian. For the non-Christian the name of God will be understood. An attentive reading of Jesus' own words in the fifth and sixth chapters of John's Gospel can give a perception of both aspects in the person of Jesus himself.

From the outset you must give attention to Christ or God in the sincere belief that God loves you—really loves you even with all of your mistakes and weaknesses, and reaches out to contact you in a living, sensible way and gently lets you recognize his presence. From the beginning we know that God is beyond all understanding, so communication will be elusive, incomplete, and, because of our weakness, seemingly sporadic. Over time you will be able to detect a change in yourself, and will become aware of a greater serenity, a more frequent awareness of God/Christ's presence during the various activities in which you engage outside of prayer time. Yet you realize that you will only find complete fulfillment in what is often called heaven or the next life.

The purpose of repeating the mantra is to maintain your consciousness of an awareness that you are in the presence of God/Christ. Sometimes this awareness will be quite perceptible. Sometimes it is an act of the understanding. Sometimes it is a stripped down act of the will. In any case, the perceptible sensing of God's presence is a mystical moment. Do not become disturbed or discouraged by repeated distractions (except those consciously chosen), but gently move away from them into awareness of Christ by using your own personal "password," your mantra. You will be strengthened by the exercise.

PRACTICE: Stop and sincerely ask God to help you decide on how to address him. Pray with your chosen mantra for a moment or two.

Lectio Divina

In addition to the mantra, another aid is what has become known over the centuries as *lectio divina* or holy reading. It is one of the most important aids to growth in contemplative or mystical prayer. You begin with the awareness of God/

Christ's presence, perhaps with the felt experience of presence. When the experience fades or is distracted, you turn to the quiet reading of scripture to maintain the connection with the sense of presence. Although the preferred source is scripture, the fathers of the Church or other spiritual reading may be used, as long as you take care to avoid purely diversionary reading: newspapers, magazines, novels, or studies, even if they have a religious orientation. You want to be intent on maintaining the presence of God and to avoid being distracted, even by the wonders of the lives of the saints or by seeking information or purely intellectual growth. Such reading is both important and beneficial, but it should be done at a separate time if you are attempting to pray the prayer of mystical presence, unless the reading truly and consciously maintains or establishes that sense of presence. There is a difference between study and mystical prayer, although either can activate the other. At this moment, however, you are seeking consciously to maintain or to reclaim union with Christ. This is why scripture is the preferred source. The Old Testament will help you to focus on God and the New Testament to reveal God in Christ.

The reading need not be long, better if it is not. It can be a word. It can be a sentence. It can be a phrase. Do not hesitate to stop reading at any moment when it suits you. Put the book down.

Gaze into space. (You may even want to close your eyes.) You are probably experiencing God/Christ's presence.

As the New Testament helps to unite one with the Christ, the Old Testament opens a source that has nurtured mystical prayer for centuries. But they can overlap. The Psalms, for example, can help in the realization of the presence of God or of Christ in the immediate present. As you continue to develop ease with mystical prayer, you may find other Old Testament sources to be very helpful. The Song of Songs, for example, has been a favorite throughout the history of Christian mysticism. In the beginning, however, it may be best to wait until you acquire a more thorough insight into the process of *exegesis* (see p. 19). Just be assured that *lectio* is a constant in the history of Christian mysticism.

PRACTICE: Open your Bible to chapter 14 of John's Gospel and read the words of Jesus in verses 15–24 as addressed to you personally. Savor them.

The Bible

$\mathcal{P}$erhaps it would be useful to insert a word here about the use of the Bible. The Old Testament presents some particular problems for you if you are relatively unfamiliar with the Bible. Reading the Old Testament may seem discouragingly complicated. Indeed, it does need study. But here we are concerned with the immediacy of prayer rather than with intellectual scholarship. We want to focus on simply maintaining conscious contact with God. Pausing here to study or research a book of the Bible, as desirable as that is at the right time, would actually be a distraction at this point. Here our goal is the conscious prayer of presence.

The Bible is a library of many literary forms. In the Old Testament you may wish to begin with some of the less complicated books, such as the Psalms, or to open to some of the prophetic literature, such as the latter part of Isaiah (beginning with chapter 40). Many people find the Wisdom Literature (sections of Job, Proverbs, Ecclesiastes, Sirach, and Wisdom) helpful. The Song of Songs also belongs among Wisdom Literature. It is the most important mystical book in the Old Testament. But hold off on that until you are a bit more familiar with the prayer of presence. Also, leave the more intricate legal and historical books for a time after you have had an opportunity to study the Bible more completely. The New Testament, of course, is basic.

Use *lectio* in the same way as you use the mantra. When God/Christ's presence is felt, that is, when you sense his nearness, do not read. Just *be*. If your awareness or attention wanders, read slowly and thoughtfully. Periodically look up and be aware of God's presence, but if your attention begins to be distracted, return to reading.

Sometimes this experience may continue for weeks. But if it is constantly interspersed even with fleeting moments in which you are aware of God's presence, it shows that you are praying and not being diverted by the attraction of growth in intellectual knowledge alone.

This experience may also apply for those who regularly pray the Liturgy of the Hours. Also known as the Divine Office, the Liturgy of the Hours serves as a guide in prayer with a community of people. When it is prayed publicly, the community of people naturally keeps moving together because individual reactions or understandings come to different individuals at different times. In private, however, you should stop when you perceive a presence. Pause as long as that presence is perceptible. It may often happen that when you pray the Liturgy of the Hours privately, you may not finish one strophe of a Psalm.

Read slowly and thoughtfully. If a phrase resonates with you, stop. Pause as long as it resonates. Sense God/Christ's presence. Remember that *lectio* is not reading purely for intellectual advance. Be relaxed as far as possible, conscious of the presence of God.

Study and prayer are two different ways to use the Bible. Both are important and one can lead to the other. From our perspective God is an inexhaustible mystery. We can study, reflect, discuss, and then study some more and never reach the point of comprehending God's vast mysteriousness. God does not expand, but our knowledge of God can and should. Prayer makes it immediate and personal; study expands our threshold of knowledge about God, and that, in turn, expands our potential for loving God. We should set aside time to study and reflect on the Ultimate Mystery on a regular basis.

It is interesting to note that in the early Church the use of the intellect led to what we call mystical prayer for some of the fathers of the Church. Their Greek classical backgrounds trained them well in the development of their intellects. In fact, even before them, who is to say that some of the ancients, like Plato, did not encounter mystical presence? His writings seem to support that possibility. The earliest Christian Greek fathers knew and studied the insights of the so-called pagan Greek philosophers to plumb the intellect for more than purely intellectual growth; they also had the wish to reach for and understand human intelligent contact with the Absolute, as a living encounter with living presence. It has often been suggested that such individuals as Plato (ca. 429–347 BC) and Plotinus (ca. 205–270 AD), a favorite of St. Augustine, were reaching for and touching the mystical. At least we can see the efforts of such thinkers as a kind of remote preparation for the astounding possibilities opened in human history by the incarnation event, which brought new and astonishing possibilities for prayer.

Thus we can see that intellectual study and the striving of the human mind and spirit can obviously be a great assistance to the development of the mystical prayer experience. It is simply necessary to remember the distinction between reading for knowledge and reading as *lectio* (an extended mantra). The two are not inimical but must be kept in proper order. There is a story about St. Teresa of Avila in which she reported that for fourteen years she found it necessary to take a book with her to prayer even if she did not open it. (That sounds like preparation for *lectio*.)

Another Greek scholar, Philo, an Alexandrian Jew who was a contemporary of St. Paul, brought the Greek contemplative ideal to an encounter with the Hebrew scriptures (Old Testament). One of his basic tools was exegesis, which was also the basic tool for mystical encounter with God/Christ for many of the early Christian scholars. It is not possible (or necessary) to delve extensively into these early remarkable Greek thinkers here, only to know that their study and use of the intellect paved the way for the earliest Christian contemplative thinkers—and pray-ers.

Knowledge and understanding can become love. Love can give greater understanding and knowledge. We have said that mystical prayer is an experience, a sensing of God/Christ's presence. Sense experience changes us, at least to some degree, into what we are sensing. We respond with love almost automatically. We should rest in it as long as possible. To repeat, the recognition and encouragement of the relationship between the will (love) and the intellect (learning) is not to belittle study; it is only to say that one's prayer time should be allowed its preeminence of place. It may be that reading a bit longer, engaging both the intellect and the affection, is still a continuance of the prayer of presence and acts as a longer mantra. The scriptural word moves the intellect to focus and the will to love, so that they experience a sense of living presence.

PRACTICE: Your Bible is important for two reasons: study and prayer. To increase the discipline of study you may wish to acquire a good basic book of scripture scholarship, such as *101 Questions and Answers on the Bible* by Raymond E. Brown (Mahwah, NJ: Paulist Press, 1990). But stop now and pray from the Bible.

Exegesis

*E*xegesis is the theological discipline that interprets and explains scripture by use of scientific methods called philology, biblical criticism and biblical history, and related sciences. It provides the spadework for scholars and even for the Church's magisterium (or teaching office), but it can be done informally by anyone. Exegesis was basic in the mystical writings of the fathers. As a matter of fact, you could say that the early theology of the Church was found in the exegesis of the scriptures by the early fathers. Consequently, when attempting to speak to mystical theology or prayer, the fathers spoke mainly exegetically. Long before theology developed as a scholastic science, there was exegesis. All early Christian theology can be called biblical theology. Therefore an understanding of exegesis is important for anyone seriously interested in pursuing mystical prayer because scripture is basic to God's revelation. This was the vehicle by which the earliest practitioners of mystical prayer found and expressed their insight. The exercise of what could be called our personal exegesis lies behind the recommendation that all *lectio* begin with scripture.

What we do when we look to encounter God/Christ in *lectio* is just that—we encounter. Strictly speaking, we are not doing exegesis in the way that scholars do. A certain degree of that will come to us personally when we study, exercising our intellect. But we are not looking for a scriptural text to illustrate or prove a point, as scholars would and must do. We are seeking an encounter with or an insight into the living Word. That Word is always available to speak to us if we are free and open.

In exegesis we apply our intellect. We try to understand. We look particularly at the context. So the encounter may be with the very first word we see on the page. It may be a phrase or a sentence. We compare a text with another similar text or look for a resonance that springs from simply reading the written word. But we try to understand it more deeply. We look for the overall situation in which the words are used and consider and compare with other words and other places in scripture. Then, we rest with it. Often we will strengthen it by returning to our mantra or making the text a kind of mantra prayer with new insight.

PRACTICE: Exegesis is like reading between the lines. Take, for example, the tenth chapter of John's Gospel about the good shepherd. Is there a meaning, beneath the familiar words *in* and *out,* about simply communing with Christ? Read it carefully and try to see things you had not considered before. How would you explain that to a friend?

Anagogy

Speaking of scripture, here is a really unusual word that addresses a little-known spiritual dynamic. It would be difficult to overstate its importance. We are not accustomed to the word, so even if we meet it in reading we might move right past it. In a way, *anagogy* moves beyond historical, allegorical, and textual exegesis. It lifts the mind and soul above the text.

Anagogy is like recognizing in the words more than the words themselves can convey: a deeper meaning, a more immediate meaning, an unexpected connection, something personal. God/Christ is speaking *to me* just as I am this minute, almost as if the words themselves are merely triggers or keys to something more that relates to me, here and now. It is as if the words themselves merely indicate, but by no means exhaust, the spoken or written subject. In themselves they cannot always do more than that because they are touching on the mystery of God who cannot be circumscribed simply by words. But there is something that resonates as very personal about it.

It is often like the note from St. Teresa of Avila quoted elsewhere and repeated here because the possible anagogic reading of scripture can have moments of insight, of presence, followed by quite ordinary moments and even by distractions:

> I used sometimes, as I have said, to experience in an elementary form, and very fleetingly, what I shall now describe. When picturing Christ in the way I have mentioned, and sometimes even when reading, I used unexpectedly to experience a consciousness of the presence of God of such a kind that I could not possibly doubt that he was within me or that I was wholly engulfed in him. This was in no sense

      a vision. I believe that it is called mystical theology.[1]

Sometimes the sense of presence will be conveyed by a small group of words but not the surrounding words.

Going in or above or beyond the written or spoken words is like passing into a different dimension, but it is in no way a contradiction of solid exegesis or the reality of this moment in time. In fact, it seems to be about this moment in time. It could be called personal rather than public. The words remain important and are read carefully, but a dimension "beyond" seems to present itself with some unmistakable clarity. God/Christ seems wonderfully perceptible with a specific insight.

Anagogy can also be seen as an understanding of the personal root or intent of the specific scripture and its implication for me right now, but it is not to be restricted to this. It presents an insight; it is another way of opening to the presence of God/Christ, often unexpectedly and quite personally. There is something immediate about it, relating to the present moment in one's life.

Origen, the earliest of the Church fathers with a distinguishing mark of genius and, so far as we

---

1. *The Life of Teresa of Jesus: The Autobiography of St. Teresa of Avila,* trans. and ed. E. Allison Peers (Garden City, NY: Doubleday Image Books, 1960), 119.

can judge, the earliest to comment methodically on the anagogical use of scripture, was certainly the most prolific in setting the pace. By the anagogic reading of scripture he seems to have meant finding something beyond the literal, the grammatical, the contextual, and the allegorical meanings to an intensifying of the person's awareness beyond, but still connected with word usages and exegetical efforts.

Origen's most intense religious experiences seem to have taken place within the work of exegesis where the soul or spirit rises momentarily beyond usual reactions to reading and learning from the word. On the one hand, he appears to be the strong proponent of the positive, cataphatic (see pp. 29 and 41) experience of God, as seen in his commentary on the erotic language of the Song of Songs. But he has speech surpassing speech itself—becoming negative or apophatic (see pp. 29 and 41)—in spite of himself. Origen is well known for his efforts in exegesis. Beyond that, it seems natural for him to expect anagogy.

PRACTICE: If you have a Bible that prints the words of Christ in red, sincerely ask God to speak to you, open the New Testament at random, and concentrate on the first words of Christ you notice as if they were being spoken personally to you.

Attitude

*A*ttitude may seem a curious subject for mystical prayer. What we are seeking in the mantra, in *lectio,* in prayer is to place ourselves as accurately as possible before, in, and with the presence of God. Our basic attitude should be that of anticipating the encounter between giver and receiver. God, the creator of all, has an essential role of giving. We creatures, on the other hand, have the essential role of receiving from God. Although it is often crowded out by thoughts of ourselves, awareness of that simple distinction is basic to prayer and one that we must strive consciously to cultivate. In even the slightest experience of the mystical prayer of presence, we feel the presence of God/Christ. We never merit the deeper experience because the divine presence is beyond what our senses and ultimately our intellect can comprehend, although we can dispose ourselves by removing evident obstacles. But the actual experience of God's closeness, no matter how brief, is not something we do or achieve through our own actions. It is a gift. Whether it is small or whether it is totally overpowering, as some mystics experienced, it is something we receive.

Even the body can be a part of this attitude or experience. To receive the presence of God you should normally place yourself in a restful bodily position—sitting, usually. Almost passively you will recognize the presence of God in this moment by faith, through images, or by simply having cleared your mind as completely as possible in order to focus on God/Christ and experience a simple sense of God's gentle presence. As you progress in this simple mystical prayer, in those moments of sensing the presence of a reality different from and beyond normal sense experience, you will feel a sense of attraction, of resonance, even of unity for those regular but brief moments. It is a feeling of gentle involvement defined by many mystical writers simply as love.

Refocusing

$\mathcal{J}$esus *is* the presence of God. The entire map of creation changed substantially when God became human. The incarnation is God's substantial physical presence in our history, world, and future. In Christ, God now has a body like ours so that he can communicate with us in a manner that is natural for us to communicate with one another. The epistle to the Hebrews begins with a clear summary statement:

> Long ago God spoke to our ancestors in many and various ways by the prophets, but in these last days he has spoken to us by a Son, whom he appointed heir of all things, through whom he also created the worlds. He is the reflection of God's glory and the exact imprint of God's very being, and he sustains all things by his powerful word. When he had made purification for sins, he sat down at the right hand of the Majesty on high. (Heb 1:1–3)

In the prayer of presence there will be times when you feel that you have mentally, emotionally, and sometimes even physically entered into God presence; at other times you may feel that God has briefly enveloped you. Sometimes the sense of presence may seem to be consciously united with Christ; at other times the presence of Christ does not seem to dominate so much as the larger experience of God. This can mean that you are so accustomed to being with Christ in your habitual prayer that your sense of God in prayer is one with Christ's sense of prayer to his Father. Christ who is so close to us by his human nature is also one with God.

PRACTICE: Put the book down. Sit quietly for a moment and be aware that God always wills to give himself to you. Focus yourself on God.

History Sketch

As already noted, a number of scholars have discerned the existence of mystical prayer before the Christian era. Certain figures in the Old Testament—Abraham, Moses (especially Moses), Jacob, and Isaiah—were all involved, in various degrees, in what today we would recognize as mystical experiences. But we have also noted that some pagan thinkers appear to have developed mystical sensibilities.

In the New Testament scholars have seen hints of mystical references in Paul and John. Paul had what many would identify as a major mystical experience that changed the entire direction of his life (see 2 Cor 12:2–4), a life that contains several other possible mystical clues. John began his Gospel with the basic recognition of the Word becoming human and continued by developing what that means.

It is good for us to be aware of historical roots. These reassure us that our experience is not simply a passing fad. Certainly to be included from the pre-Christian Greek world are Plato (ca. 429–347 BC), Plotinus (205–270), and Philo (a Jewish contemporary of Christ, the first to combine Greek wisdom with exegesis of the Hebrew scriptures). Then, outstanding in early Christian history is Origen (ca.185–254) who suggested that we have spiritual senses for understanding the anthropomorphic language of the Bible (i.e., language that speaks of God in human images).

After Origen came Gregory of Nyssa (335–395) who first addressed the periods of darkness in prayer, and Evagrius Ponticus (ca. 345–399) who expanded on the relationship among the intellect, contemplation, and asceticism in prayer and directed more thought to the root mystery of the Trinity. Later, the mysterious Dionysius (ca. 500) explored apophatic, that is, negative, prayer (and cataphatic, that is, positive, prayer). Pope Gregory the Great (540–604) sought the balance between action and contemplation. The astonishing but, until our own time, largely overlooked Eriugena (ca. 815–877) revived Platonic thought. All these mystics paved the way for that remarkable figure, Bernard of Clairvaux (1090–1153). Bernard went beyond Origen's spiritual senses to say that mystical prayer involves the action of the full human experience, both carnal and spiritual, ultimately as a single sensation.

The Middle Ages saw the rise of such familiar figures as Thomas Aquinas (1225–1274) and Meister Eckhart (1260–1328) whose thought influenced the later world of well-known mystics such as John of the Cross (1542–1591) and Teresa of Avila (1515–1582) and still others of our own day and time.

These are simply representative names from a long and developing history. In personal *lectio* these writers may be good sources to accompany the Bible as long as we keep in mind that they were dealing with conditions in a world very different from our own and acknowledge that the Bible should always hold the place of prominence.

Moving On

Christ remains the base and the avenue of Christian prayer. Consciousness of trying to live in him will, sooner or later, become more effortless so that we are united with him in his relationship with the Father in the Spirit, and we simply sense awareness of presence even at unexpected moments.

Use the mantra while it is useful, but do not become so bound to it that the mind is more occupied with it than with simple awareness of God. The sense of the presence of God/Christ is always paramount. There will come times when even the simple mantra is not necessary to cultivate an awareness of God's presence. Rather, that awareness replaces an introductory use of the mantra. Gradually the experience of presence moderates all of life, even though not always consciously. You will find that a basic sense of serenity is increasingly governing not only your times of prayer, but all your life situations. At times of stress or difficulty, a conscious recalling of God/Christ's presence moderates what would otherwise be dominated by concern, worry, or discomfort.

It cannot be stressed too often that contemplative and mystical prayer is rooted in the experience of God's presence. It does not ultimately rely on words, images, or actions but on awareness of God's love. In this sense, such prayer could be called more passive than active. The emotions and the intellect generally need not be consciously involved. To sense God/Christ's presence may generate an emotion or bring about an understanding—for example, calmness and serenity and a sense of personal fulfillment as a kind of side effect to the most difficult and trying situation—but this is not the essence of prayer, which is quiet in God's presence. We may easily imagine that Jesus must have prayed in that way in those times when he went to the mountain alone. Scripture is silent on how he prayed there, and perhaps he was simply silent with his Father. It is evident that this silence and solitude are important to mystical prayer.

PRACTICE: Do not ever allow yourself to be overcome with discouragement. It may be just a challenge to exercise and develop your faith more completely.

Darkness and Night

One of the things that has often discouraged many a sincere beginner, or even a seasoned pray-er, is apprehension about the "dark night" of the soul or the senses. This dark night is often misunderstood as a positive force that burdens a person with suffering as a specific stage that must be experienced before advancing in prayer. But that is not what it is; rather, it is a sense of absence, of missing the sense of God/Christ's perceptible presence.

Even Jesus experienced times when his Father's presence seemed to be obscured. This is emphasized in his sense of aloneness during his agony in the garden the night before he died and his heart-wrenching cry of abandonment from the cross.

Perhaps surprisingly, the sense of absence and presence can coexist. Mystics through the ages have described this as "dryness," "darkness," "night," "desert," "aridity," and "distraction." What has been called "heroic sanctity" is often marked by the constancy of faith in God/Christ's presence even when it is achieved and sustained almost totally by will power in faith without the balm of more sensitive perception. But the prayer of faith is often its own reassurance and stimulates a certain serenity of presence.

This is a very important crossroad in the progress of prayer. We have said that it is a point of serious discouragement for many who too often misunderstand it as a torturous stage that must be endured before they can advance to the next stage. So it is crucial to begin to understand it. It is not so much a stage of progress or a one-time hurdle that must be met and conquered before further growth can take place, as it is a recurrent experience that may vary greatly in length. The term *darkness* is known from the writings of the sixteenth-century Spanish mystic St. John of the Cross, who spoke of "the dark night." John, however, very likely learned the term from the writings of St. Gregory of Nyssa, an early fourth-century father of the Church who wrote extensively about the life of Moses. Gregory saw Moses progressing through three stages in his spiritual life, terminating at the mountain when he passes through the cloud to experience God directly in an encounter apparently ineffably (indescribably) beyond sense knowledge or cognitional definition. Because sense and intellect are inadequate or absent, he calls the absence of their light "darkness." Read the experience of Moses in the book of Exodus (32—34), and note that the final "stage" of experience is not before but with the final stage of presence or darkness.

It would be a mistake to think that God somehow becomes absent in times of aridity. God is always present but is perceived differently, without the same help from the emotions or even the intellect. To judge the sense of presence by emotion or by reason is to draw the line of perception too low. God/Christ is also perceived by faith. Faith is a third way of knowing beyond emotion and reason. The night or darkness is not abandonment or withdrawal by God. Presence is still perceptible. It is different. In a way it may be nearer the mystery of God's own self-communication. And it can be an important growing time. Muscles must be exercised to grow strong. This experience can be an exercise of "spiritual muscles." It becomes more elusive and grows beyond the ability to describe, yet it remains somewhat perceptible by the consciousness of faith.

Nor is darkness in this understanding to be confused with clinical or psychic depression as identified by contemporary psychology, although sometimes these conditions may be attendant. There are times and events in life when we suffer from a great sadness, pain, despondency, or depression and do not initially sense the more immediate presence of God. This is not darkness in the same sense but the combination of circumstances that clearly create a condition that may make it seem so. Even when things are at their lowest we can, by the will, hold on to the faith that God is lovingly present. Dionysius even speaks of "the dazzling darkness of hidden silence" and sees darkness itself as a form of prayer. He wrote:

> The fact is that the more we take flight upward, the more our words are confined to the ideas we are capable of forming; so that now as we plunge into that darkness which is beyond intel-

lect, we shall find ourselves not simply running short of words but actually speechless and unknowing.[2]

It is basically a consciousness of fidelity in recognizing God/Christ's presence that reaches beyond the bodily senses and power of reasoning. God in his essence is so far removed from our capacity to comprehend or sense that God's indefinable mystery seems dark compared to what we perceive in the light of the human situation around us or to previous, more emotional and intellectually satisfying instances of awareness of God's presence.

Uncertainty, darkness, and apparent absence at some juncture should not be surprising. Nor should it be feared. God loves us. We love God. God's presence has not left us; it is, for the time being, different.

In many ways we can see this experience as an intensification or growth in our relationship with God, something God gives us but, because we are still growing and free, something we must accept and believe in order to benefit. It is a way of recognizing God's presence in the midst of other affairs of daily living and encounter with neighbors when we are very busy, distracted, sad, alone, or ill.

---

2. Dionysius, *The Mystical Theology*, quoted in *Light from Light*, ed. Louis Dupré and James A. Wiseman, OSB, 2nd ed. (Mahwah, NJ: Paulist Press, 2001), 89–90.

The unknown fourteenth-century English mystic who wrote *The Cloud of Unknowing* encouraged his readers by writing:

> And so diligently persevere until you feel joy in it. For in the beginning it is usual to feel nothing but a kind of darkness about our mind, or as it were, *a cloud of unknowing*. You will seem to know nothing and to feel nothing except a naked intent toward God in the depths of your being. Try as you might, this darkness and this cloud will remain between you and your God. You will feel frustrated, for your mind will be unable to grasp him, and your heart will not relish the delight of his love. But learn to be at home in this darkness. Return to it as often as you can, letting your spirit cry out to him whom you love. For if, in this life, you hope to feel and see God as he is in himself it must be within this darkness and this cloud. But if you strive to fix your love on him forgetting all else, which is the work of contemplation I have urged you to begin, I am confident that God in his goodness will

bring you to a deep experience of himself.[3]

And a passage from the Letter to the Ephesians may also be helpful here:

> I pray that, according to the riches of his glory, he may grant that you may be strengthened in your inner being with power through his Spirit and that Christ may dwell in your hearts through faith, as you are being rooted and grounded in love. I pray that you may have the power to comprehend, with all the saints, what is the breadth and length and height and depth, and to know the love of Christ that surpasses knowledge, so that you may be filled with all the fullness of God. (Eph 3:16–19)

PRACTICE: We all have times of darkness. You may be having one now. Let your mind believe God's presence to you even if you do not feel that presence. You will begin to notice a different kind of presence-in-depth based on faith alone. Have I thought the dark night is a prolonged event or experience?

---

3. *The Cloud of Unknowing*, ed. William Johnston (New York: Doubleday, 1973), 48–49.

Should I not rather see it as an intermittent challenge I need to transform into a higher, stronger form of prayer to sustain me especially during difficulties?

Growth

*D*o not expect miracles of change. Any kind of growth usually happens rather quietly and unnoticed until suddenly you realize there has been a change in size, shape, color, and, with humans, wisdom. Think of a garden in early spring and its stages of growth. And then think of growth in this kind of prayer similarly. You must be patient, full of hope and expectancy.

At times the sense of presence is so strong that your whole being seems immersed in an experience that cannot be described. It is usually relatively short but leaves you with an attitude of serenity and quiet wonder, and its effects can be immediate and then, with time, it becomes quietly transformative.

What can be said of the experience itself? Remember that experiential awareness of the presence of God/Christ may come during prayer or unexpectedly. This does not mean that your own efforts will produce the experience. Rather, efforts to pray dispose you to be open and sensitive to the experience when it occurs.

Is this experience only for a few chosen people? No. There was a time, especially during and following the Middle Ages, when any mystical experience seemed to be considered almost the achievement of spiritual effort in a long process by people who were practically heroes and heroines. Yet, even children can experience the presence of God, as attested by Jesus himself.

There is almost always a wish to describe or share the experience of God's presence. But even the greatest mystics have found that an impossibility. Earlier we read about the great mystic St. Teresa of Avila's attempt to describe her experiences (see p. 22). Her great contemporary, St. John of the Cross, could only resort to poetic language and still find it inadequate.

PRACTICE: Stop and think. Am I willing to be patient? With faith?

Basic Types of Mystical Prayer

*T*here are two classical ways to speak of general types of mystical prayer. The words to identify them are not in the common vocabulary of most people, but are still used in the works of scholars and in Christian history. At present they are the only words that can adequately recognize the realities discussed. Today they are becoming more commonly understood as mystical prayer grows in wider understanding. The words are *cataphatic* and *apophatic* and they are Greek words meaning positive and negative.

Cataphatic prayer is prayer that employs thoughts and images in our communication with God. One well-known proponent of cataphatic prayer was St. Ignatius of Loyola. His *Spiritual Exercises* use reason, will, imagination, feelings, and senses in prayer in order to communicate with the Lord by the sharing of thoughts and feelings. The best source for cataphatic prayer is scripture.

Apophatic prayer, on the other hand, is a kind of prayer in which one learns to be comfortable with God beyond all thoughts and images. The author of the fourteenth-century spiritual master-piece *The Cloud of Unknowing* suggests that one way of getting into this prayer is to choose a single word—a mantra—and then reject any thought, image, or feeling that the word may generate so that your attention will be centered exclusively on the reality beyond that word. In this type of prayer we seek to transcend our conscious awareness and to reach the depths of our being in which we meet the Lord. There is a self-emptying in the presence of God who is far beyond our ability ever to comprehend.

How are cataphatic and apophatic prayer related to each other? We might say that they are complementary. Cataphatic prayer aims to evoke God's love and mercy and to deepen our knowledge of and union with Christ. Apophatic prayer, on the other hand, seeks union with God beyond conscious awareness. One type of prayer does not necessarily lead to the other (although it may), nor is either one in any way superior to the other. Each is a means of encountering the Lord in prayer, and which one you choose will be the one with which you feel most comfortable.

PRACTICE: Stop for a moment and briefly try to pray both ways. Have a mental picture of Christ stilling the waves of a troubled and frightening sea. Perhaps say a word to him. Then try to push all images out of your mind and simply be aware that you are in his calming presence.

A Quiet Gift

*T*he experience of God is ineffable—beyond words, often brief, and often unexpected. Familiarity with Jesus and his life–death–resurrection can be understood as a beginning of being present with him and in him through the events or mysteries of his life. Concrete meditation on the events of Christ's life can focus and refocus us. Then, without even further use of gospel images and words, we might unexpectedly rest in his ineffable presence. That is an illustration of the cataphatic and apophatic dynamic working together.

How do you know that you are moving in the right direction? This concern has been with disciples from the beginning. At the Last Supper Thomas asked the Lord, "How can we know the way" (John 14:5), to which Jesus responded simply, "I am the way" (John 14:6). Jesus did not respond with directions, a map, an outline, or a book. The person of Christ is the Way.

No one pursues mystical prayer as an accomplishment to be merited and won. It is always a gift. You only dispose yourself to receive it. The most that you can do is to prepare the way for that deeper union with God/Christ in all aspects of your life. If Karl Rahner was correct, however, we all have mystical moments and the matter then becomes one of recognizing, entering, responding to, and nurturing them. Do not expect crashing cymbals or blaring trumpets. God comes gently and quietly. But believe the experience.

Oneness or Commotion?

In the beginning and during periods of dryness, darkness, or distraction, recalling your mantra during your prayer time is usually helpful in sustaining a sense of God's presence. Know, however, that God is present everywhere— here, around you, in you. If unexpected circumstances occur to disrupt your normal prayer schedule, even a brief prayer (an awareness of presence if possible; if not, a simple focused prayer of the will) can be offered to maintain your daily pattern of receptive prayer.

One problem we might encounter is a sense of loss of contact with divine presence. Here we might borrow a pair of words from the Jewish philosopher Martin Buber (1878–1965) who spoke of a sense of "commotion" over against a sense of "oneness." According to Buber, mysticism that isolates the individual from the world is not an ideal. Mystical prayer must be combined with action in service to the world. This caution appears with regularity in the Christian writers, including the mystics. Contemplation without openness to serving others can be an exercise in selfishness and the termination of true mystical experience.

This basic concept serves well in the effort to come to terms with distractions or perceived failures in maintaining a prayerful awareness of God's presence. If we allow such commotions to predominate and become exclusive, they can easily overcome us. But Buber would also be concerned if what he called oneness or union were to predominate to the exclusion of the world outside. Not only is the incarnational mystery ignored, but also the possibility of experiencing God's presence in creation where God often unpredictably touches us is compromised. The full picture recognizes both the commotion and oneness but sees the commotion rooted in and directed by the oneness.

PRACTICE: Stop for a moment and think: Is my prayer more truly described by oneness or by commotion?

Assurance

What ongoing assurance can we find that we are moving in the right direction? Jesus said, "You will know them by their fruits" (Matt 7:16). If we regularly experience a sense of God/Christ's presence or simply recognize and embrace it with our will, the fruit is already there. The fruit is also discernible if our attitude toward life in general begins to become more peaceful. This resonates with the saying that the medieval English mystic Julian of Norwich repeats like a mantra in any uncertainty or difficulty: "All will be well."

The American philosopher and experimental psychologist William James, in his classic work *The*

Varieties of Religious Experience, offers a few concrete and practical signs of assurance. In his words the central ones are:

> – the loss of all worry, the sense that all is ultimately well with one, the peace, the harmony the *willingness to be,* even though the outer condition should remain the same.
> – the sense of perceiving truths not known before. The mysteries of life become lucid.
> – the objective change which the world often appears to undergo. An appearance of newness beautifies every object.[4]

James sees these as assurances found in a conversion experience. Mystical prayer is a constant conversion process, a process of growing nearer and nearer the presence and experience of God/Christ. To the extent that they mirror the experience of ongoing prayer, these assurances are a kind of hallmark as well as a reminder for living in awareness of divine presence being communicated to us. This

---

4. William James, *The Varieties of Religious Experience,* The Modern Library (New York: Random House, 1929), 242–43.

is another way of describing the heart and environment of contemplative mystical prayer.

PRACTICE: Read William James's assurances again and see if you can identify with one or all of them.

Joy

*T*he encounter with God inevitably brings joy! You sense that even the features of your face relax into a quiet smile. Peace and joy coalesce. There is quietness and total absorption—even if only for a moment or two. You want to continue in this state but are soon distracted, then possibly reoriented briefly. You would like to remember, to describe. It is too elusive. But remembering the peaceful joy of the experience can help to reestablish contact. Take note of the words of St. Paul:

> Rejoice in the Lord always; again, I will say, Rejoice. Let your gentleness be

known to everyone. The Lord is near. Do not worry about anything, but in everything by prayer and supplication with thanksgiving let your requests be made known to God. And the peace of God, which surpasses all understanding, will guard your hearts and your minds in Christ Jesus. (Phil 4:4–7)

Time—The Now

The heart of mystical prayer is the now. This minute, this quarter hour, this time is completely directed to and immersed in our presence to God and God's presence to us. Time seems momentarily stopped. Everything else falls away. You rest in presence "with." The experience is joy and peace and fulfillment. It is now. A child once observed to his father, "But, there is no present moment. This moment has already passed or the next moment has not yet arrived." Perhaps in that infinitesimal space between moments we touch upon eternity where time is no more. The mystery of that elusive present is a focus on the now. The present relates to presence—the sense of being with God who is the eternal Now—so the present moment can hold a secret, an entry into eternal presence. How, then, does one maximize that present, that now? It is not unlike what the Buddhist tradition calls *attentiveness*—not looking back, not looking forward, merely attending to the now. Buddhists are known to spend periods of time merely attending to a flower blossom. If that discipline of attentiveness were directed not only to an object, but also to the experience of the presence of the eternal God/Christ, what might be the result? You must remain quiet, peaceful, calm, and radically joyful. This joy, however, cannot usually become ebullient, demonstrative, or excited, or it will become distraction.

There is another facet of time that sometimes applies: memory. Memory touches on a powerful reality. This should be no surprise for the Christian. It is pivotal for belief in the Eucharist. Remembering and responding to Jesus' instruction to "do this in remembrance of me" (Luke 22:19), not only recalls a past historical event but also represents it in the paschal mystery for communal celebration. For private or personal remembrance apart from the liturgy it sometimes helps to re-orient oneself to a previous experience of God's presence. Remembrance has a way of making present, even if briefly, a past experience. It is more than simply recalling.

It is like reestablishing a point of contact that may once again come alive.

PRACTICE: Stop and try to experience just this moment as presence with God.

Solitude and Activity

Is it necessary to withdraw totally from the world to find the ground for mystical prayer? No. In fact, an honest and careful look at history reveals that most of the great mystics have spoken clearly against a complete withdrawal from the world. Some of the greatest mystical authors, such as Gregory the Great and Bernard of Clairvaux, admit that even for them it was a continuous personal struggle. Gregory, a monk when he became pope, encountered the "action versus contemplation" dilemma head-on and clearly identified the two dimensions. Bernard's life was a constant mix of both action in the world and contemplation in the monastery. The "versus" should not indicate an either/or dichotomy but should rather be seen as dealing with a both/and necessity. One should keep in mind, however, that both men were monks with strong monastic ties. When action got the best of them they hungered for the quiet, the solitude they had found in their monasteries. And their writings reflect that. Admiring Bernard very highly, we would like to reassure some of his worries that loving union with Christ/God can also be found outside the monastery. Bernard sees the call to contemplation offered to all Christians theoretically, but that it is very difficult, if not impossible, for anyone outside the monastery to attain the contemplative presence of God/Christ. He was very much a person of his age, and an unusually active monk outside the cloister, finding refreshment when he could stay home and give contemplation more undivided attention. And, perhaps it is more difficult to experience this higher stage of union with God/Christ in the hyper-charged distractions of the everyday world. But this is not necessarily so for the ordinary conscious experiences of presence in mystical prayer. Call it "mystical prayer in simple form" or something similar. It is more than an intellectual act of faith that one can sustain without the experience. The sense, the experience, can be concretely perceptible, even if brief and elusive. Most great men and women of mysticism have spoken and acted clearly against an absolute withdrawal from the world while they personally preferred the contemplative and mystical life. The common and erroneous belief that mysticism is a flight from the world may derive from the idea that religion and spirituality are a strictly private affair or must be conducted behind hermit-like or monastic walls. How were the "common people" meeting the same challenge? By and large, they could not write so we know very little first hand.

We should remember that Anthony of Egypt, often cited as the "first hermit," more than once found it necessary to leave his solitude in response to the call to more public ministry. Bernard's uneasy struggle with the tension between action and contemplation was exacerbated by the potential for a dualism developing in much medieval theology. This dualism separated theory and practice, body and spirit, spiritual and worldly, the contemplative and active life, and found its scriptural basis in an overemphasized contrast between Martha and Mary in the New Testament:

> Now as they went on their way, he [Jesus] entered a certain village, where a woman named Martha welcomed him into her home. She had a sister named Mary, who sat at the Lord's feet and listened to what he was saying. But Martha was distracted by her many tasks; so she came to him and asked, "Lord, do you not care that my sister has left me to do

all the work by myself? Tell her then to help me." But the Lord answered her, "Martha, Martha, you are worried and distracted by many things; there is need of only one thing. Mary has chosen the better part, which will not be taken away from her." (Luke 10:38–42)

Mystics like Teresa of Avila ultimately criticized this tendency and brought about a reform. Teresa pointed out that it took both action and contemplation together to host the Lord and keep him. The active and contemplative dimensions need each other, even in the individual person.

Although a certain discipline of life is necessary, a psychologically forced attendance to prayer time in solitude is often a bad sign. If we look forward to prayer, it is often a good sign that we are on the right way. If prayer time is simply a duty performed, we have not really tasted the experience of presence. We should honestly want to return to prayer, not feel obliged to observe it.

PRACTICE: Ask yourself: Do I wonder whether I am more like Martha or Mary when I should be seriously trying to recognize both in my life?

From Contemplation to Action and Back Again

*T*he attraction of God/Christ's presence is not limited to one religious tradition. It certainly is not limited to the hermit's hut or the cloister walls. Because God is God, his love is not limited. And if God loves all, all should be able to experience his love. All creatures that possess intellect and emotions should be able to receive, sense, and have contact with God. This means, of course, that such experiences are as varied as people are varied.

In mystical prayer, this experience, even if brief, becomes pivotal. It may become more than an isolated moment. Receptiveness to that presence is hidden in me yet is enveloping me. I must discover it. I must find it. I am helped to do so by occasional unexpected mystical moments, to use Rahner's term. I may not immediately recognize them as God events, though I am aware that there is something unusual or special about the moment or sensation. Reflection will bring such an experience to conscious recognition.

For some, in certain special, unusual instances, mystical prayer may include visions and other extraordinary sensory perceptions. This is not normative or necessary. For most, it will not be anything so dramatic. It will be a simple, gentle sense of presence often resonating something like the experience of Elijah recorded in the Old Testament:

> He said, "Go out and stand on the mountain before the LORD, for the LORD is about to pass by." Now there was a great wind, so strong that it was splitting mountains and breaking rocks in pieces before the LORD, but the LORD was not in the wind; and after the wind an earthquake, but the LORD was not in the earthquake; and after the earthquake a fire, but the LORD was not in the fire; and after the fire a sound of sheer silence. When Elijah heard it, he wrapped his face in his mantle and went out and stood at the entrance of the cave. Then there came a voice to him that said, "What are you doing here Elijah?" (1 Kgs 19:11–13)

We might ask ourselves the same question and recognize God's answer in a simple whisper!

To receive these divine initiatives one must, at least for a moment, be reasonably quiet. These initiatives occur even in childhood and youth, often are forgotten, but can at least to a degree be stirred by memory. And memory can open the door for a reawakening or development of experience. The power of memory is often unrecognized, yet it is established as a powerful reality in both Jewish and Christian theology and liturgy. Remembrance can also make present the connection with mystery and presence. To view our experiences as trivial or not worthy of further consideration often blocks the way to understanding them fully and can slow growth and development in prayer.

This is also an indication that contemplative, mystical prayer is not only for a chosen few, or for a specialized elite who are "different," as many of the medieval stories of mystics seem to imply. St. John of the Cross, himself a mystic, said explicitly the contrary that "God is willing that all should embrace this high calling of contemplation, but finds few who permit him to work such sublime things for them."[5]

And so we sit. We are quiet and still. We try to empty the mind of thought or worry, simply resting quietly and becoming aware that we are in God's presence. Perhaps we quietly speak the name of Jesus to ourselves.

Then there comes an interruption—a time for work, for eating, for ministry to others. Time to leave our quiet space. Is this truly an interruption?

5. Quoted in Dorothee Soelle, *The Silent Cry: Mysticism and Resistance*, trans. Barbara Rumscheidt and Martin Rumscheidt (Minneapolis: Fortress Press, 2001), 14.

Is this "too much Martha" and "not enough Mary"? As we have already noted, this has seemed to present a quandary for people who are serious about growth in prayer and yet called to activity apart from a monastery, convent, solitude, silence, and a quiet place. Are these two conflicting forces or is integration possible?

Recall what was said earlier about Gregory the Great and Bernard of Clairvaux. Their active lives were clearly important, yet both confessed to a persistent yearning to return to the monasteries they had left. Was this a message to leave the active life and reclaim the more sheltered contemplative way? Or was it a kind of nostalgia for a better time in the past than the complicated time in the present? Or, conversely, let us ask why Anthony of Egypt felt pulled more than once to leave his solitude to respond to the expressed needs of others.

Does it need to be an either/or situation? Can it not, very often should it not, be a both/and situation—not as a compromise but as a recognized call from God in Christ? Sometimes it seems as if the lines have been drawn too severely, and the monastic ideal has created a psychological and spiritual inferiority complex for a form of life that is normative for the majority of people.

It is an age-old quandary for anyone trying to juxtapose elements of a more perfect life. We must then examine the both/and possibility more seriously. Let us go back even beyond Gregory, Bernard, and Anthony to the earliest part of the Old Testament where we can encounter Moses as more than a people's leader-out-of captivity and find in him a figure often quoted in mystical literature. Moses' life seems almost an epitome of a molding of the active and contemplative lifestyles. One of the earliest Christians to note this and write about it is the man we have already credited for developing an understanding of the meaning of darkness in the life of prayer—Gregory of Nyssa. In his *Life of Moses*, after speaking of his conscious union with God especially in darkness he writes:

> Made to desire and not to abandon the transcendent height by things already attained, it makes its way upward without ceasing, ever through its prior accomplishments renewing its intensity for flight. *Activity* directed toward virtue causes its capacity to grow through exertion; this kind of activity alone does not slacken its intensity by effort, but increases it.[6]

To prove his point, Gregory then details a list of various activities Moses engaged in while main-

---

6. Gregory of Nyssa, *Life of Moses*, quoted in *Light from Light*, 50.

taining what we would call his mystical/contemplative presence with and to God:

> He avenged the Hebrew...he shepherded a flock of tame animals; he saw the brilliance of the light; unencumbered, having taken off his sandals, he made his approach to the light; he brought his kinsmen and countrymen out to freedom; he saw the enemy drowning in the sea; he made camps under the cloud; he quenched thirst from the rock; he produced bread from heaven; by stretching out his hands, he overcame the foreigner; he heard the trumpet; he entered the darkness.[7]

Yet, with all this activity Moses is recognized as virtually the primordial mystic.

We need only to remind ourselves regularly that action is undertaken in love, but that time is conserved for the prayer of presence. And, as return to the mantra is helpful in prayer times, the mantra can also help us during action times. This can be seen variously in the lives of such individuals as Francis of Assisi and Thérèse of Lisieux, who, in spite of her life in Carmelite seclusion, had such a

---

7. Ibid., 228–29.

love for the activity of the missions and so wished to go out herself that she has officially received the title "Patroness of the Missions." Was the scientifically active Pierre Teilhard de Chardin a mystic in our own time?

The supreme example, however, is Christ himself. There can be no doubt about action in the life and ministry of the Word Incarnate. The Gospels are full of illustrations of his activity. Yet, apart from giving the disciples a simple formula for prayer (the Our Father), we know little about Christ's contemplative (and certainly mystical) personal prayer. We only know that he regularly made significant time for it and sought places of solitude for it. Yet, we can only surmise the content of that prayer. No words are recorded for his prayer on the mountain or in a desert place except briefly, for example in the garden on the night before he died, as noted in the Synoptic Gospels. And we should keep in mind that these specially noted prayer times occurred during a very active life. He did, however, recommend quiet and solitude when he advised his disciples:

> "And whenever you pray, do not be like the hypocrites; for they love to stand and pray in the synagogues and at the street corners, so that they may be seen by others. Truly I tell you, they have

received their reward. But whenever you pray, go into your room and shut the door and pray to your Father who is in secret; and your Father who sees in secret will reward you." (Matt 6:5–6)

No matter how personal and individual the mystical prayer of presence is, one can never lose sight of love for the community to which one belongs.

PRACTICE: Ask yourself how you combine action and contemplation on a regular basis in your life. Does it need adjusting? Tell Christ. Make a resolution.

Beauty

True beauty, in nature or in the arts, can bring one to the threshold of the prayer of presence. It can move almost effortlessly from a brief cataphatic encounter to a brief apophatic experience, beyond the purely physical encounter.

The immediate cataphatic lever can be any number of things, such as a sunset, a painting, a poem, a symphony, or a landscape.

Gregory of Nyssa makes this quite clear:

> Such an experience seems to me to belong to the soul that loves what is beautiful. Hope always draws the soul from the beauty that is seen to what is beyond, always kindles the desire for the hidden through what is constantly perceived. Therefore, the ardent lover of beauty, although receiving what is always visible as an image of what he desires, yet longs to be filled with the very stamp of the archetype.[8]

A similar experience elicited the famous exclamation of Augustine in his *Confessions*:

> Late have I loved you, O Beauty, so ancient and so new, late have I loved you! And behold, you were within me and I was outside, and there I sought for you, and in my deformity I rushed headlong into the well-formed things that you have made. You were with me,

---

8. Gregory of Nyssa, *Life of Moses,* quoted in *Light from Light,* 51.

and I was not with you. Those outer beauties held me far from you, yet if they had not been in you, they would not have existed at all. You called and cried out to me and broke open my deafness; you shone forth upon me and you scattered my blindness; you breathed fragrance, and I drew in my breath and I now pant for you; I tasted and I hunger and thirst; you touched me, and I burned for your peace.[9]

It was probably insights like these that urged Hans Urs von Balthasar to pursue his conviction that beauty is one of the transcendentals in theology along with Aquinas's threefold listing of unity, truth, and goodness. (Transcendentals in the study of theology and philosophy are properties that belong to a being simply because it is a being, transcending [i.e., going beyond] qualities like time and space.)

You must be prepared and let yourself be drawn through physical beauty into sensing the everlasting beauty of the conscious experience of God/Christ.

---

9. Augustine, *The Confessions*, quoted in *Light from Light*, 62.

PRACTICE: Think of something that represents beauty to you—a painting, a piece of music, a photograph of a beloved person or breathtaking scenery, for example. How does this source of beauty make God present to you?

St. Paul and St. John

The Incarnation is the paradigm for bringing together the active and contemplative/mystical life. As we proceed in prayer, an increasingly closer identification with the person of Jesus naturally develops. Meditation on the life of Christ becomes a source of growth. Meditation on his life—cataphatic prayer—and the insights of St. Paul and St. John into the mysteries of that life provide a solid basis of union with Christ. Paul's concept of "identification with Christ" carries a consistent echo in the history of mysticism. It makes an awareness of Christ habitual. All things and everything attempts to center around a consciousness of that awareness.

This can occur in one's conscious prayer *to* Christ since one is praying, experiencing the presence of God *with* Christ, *in* Christ, and *by means* of Christ. We experience the presence of God at least somewhat as he does, and with him, even if not to the same degree. After Paul's famous encounters with Christ (see 1 Cor 9:1; 15:8; and Acts 9:1–9; 15:8), Paul became such a changed man that in his letters the simple phrase "in Christ" occurs 164 times! It is the pivotal focus of Pauline spirituality. We are in Christ. He is in us. We can sense his presence if we but open the shutters of emotion and reason and believe, concretely, that he is in us, praying. He is always praying with and is conscious of the Father and Spirit since he, as Logos, is one with them. At some point this awareness becomes available to us and we feel it. We are caught up in being aware of God's presence with and in Christ. And he in us. That is mystical prayer.

In Paul's case it reached the height described by Paul himself:

> I know a person in Christ who fourteen years ago was caught up to the third heaven—whether in the body or out of the body I do not know; God knows. And I know that such a person— whether in the body or out of the body I do not know; God knows—was caught

up into Paradise and heard things that
are not to be told, that no mortal is per-
mitted to repeat. (2 Cor 12:2–4)

Paul's description seems to describe what we would
call a mystical experience.

John provides the most concise and yet lyri-
cal recognition of the Incarnation event in the introductory phrases to both his Gospel and his First
Letter. Here is the prologue to his Gospel:

In the beginning was the Word, and the
Word was with God, and the Word was
God. He was in the beginning with
God. All things came into being
through him, and without him not one
thing came into being. What has come
into being in him was life, and the life
was the light of all people. The light
shines in the darkness, and the darkness did not overcome it….And the
Word became flesh and lived among
us, and we have seen his glory, the
glory as of a father's only son, full of
grace and truth. (John 1:1–5, 14)

The concreteness of the Incarnation is expressed
again in the opening to the First Letter of John:

We declare to you what was from the beginning, what we have heard, what we have seen with our eyes, what we have looked at and touched with our hands, concerning the word of life— this life was revealed, and we have seen it and testify to it, and declare to you the eternal life that was with the Father and was revealed to us—we declare to you what we have seen and heard so that you also may have fellowship with us; and truly our fellowship is with the Father and with his Son Jesus Christ. (1 John 1:1–3)

If we stop to allow ourselves to be conscious of Christ's presence even in the midst of action, that too is mystical prayer.

PRACTICE: Why not stop reading this book and pause a moment with each of these readings? Or with just one of them? Take the words as addressed to you personally, now, at this moment.

Image and Likeness

The book of Genesis tells us we are made in the image and likeness of God. We keep searching for that rootedness, and the mystery of the incarnation makes it more possible for us to find it. God is the ultimate mystery. Because of the incarnation we know that God's inner life is a Trinity: Father, Son (or Word or Image), and Spirit. We believe that Christ is the image of the invisible God (see Col 1:15), God "made flesh," revealed in scripture. Because of sin, however, the likeness is often clouded or veiled. We slowly remove the veil and clear the cloud by our efforts to make our own personal image increasingly reflect the Image that is the Word, the Son.

The hunger to find communion with God is in our nature. Human history is an unfolding story of efforts to do so. This is evident even from the rudimentary archeological finds of the most ancient human past on through the great masters of all time. In Western civilization this was already becoming more evident in Greek history with the efforts of great seekers of the truth like Plato (ca. 429–347 BC) and those touched by his probing mind. From them we hear of "the Absolute" surprisingly described in various trinitarian formats: goodness/

knowledge/beauty, or being/life/intellect, or faith/truth/love, or being/intellect/will, and various other trinitarian formulae for one Absolute Being. Finally, Jesus specifically identified that eternal internal reality as Father/Son (or Word)/Spirit and identified himself as the Son or Word now become incarnate.

So, because of human sin and weakness our likeness finds itself cloudy. Yet, it labors to bring itself into conformity with its original portrait whose image it bears. We will never completely achieve this in our lifetime, but the progress toward the goal may continue, increase, and improve. That is why we pray (and work). And that is also why the experience of God's presence is not something unusual or necessarily rare, but is sometimes difficult to identify and maintain. Access is through Christ, because by the Incarnation, God has been made physically present in a human body like ours. And the Trinity in Christ has come and lived among us. We, in turn, find a greatly enhanced possibility of improving the likeness of that image in ourselves.

PRACTICE: If our language about God seems difficult and demanding, remember we are just talking about God. God will always remain the greatest of mysteries, beyond our words.

Liturgy

*T*hroughout the history of Christian mystical prayer there is a connection with the liturgy and sacramental life of the Church. This is cataphatic in nature, but may become the vehicle of being lifted apophatically to God. True mystical prayer is never completely private or individualistic. It is therefore not only good but important to keep in mind the words of the Second Vatican Council that the liturgy is the "source" and "summit" of prayer. It is the same principle that motivates the consistent urge to find the proper proportion between action and contemplation evident in some of the great figures in history, such as Gregory the Great and Bernard of Clairvaux.

Here is a way to look at it. After his ascension into heaven, Christ is still made sacramentally accessible here on earth through Word and Eucharist in the worship of the Christian community. Our liturgy is a communal recognition, acceptance, and celebration of Christ's continuing presence among us.

The life of Christian prayer will always contain communal worship, sacraments, and eucharistic action. Private or individual prayer is not sufficient. It is almost like saying that God had to become Incarnate for us to touch him. We have bodies. And it is only by using our bodies with our minds that we will find access to God, though we may often feel lost along the way. Mystical prayer is both cataphatic and apophatic. We use physical things and we rise beyond them. Even in periods of darkness, the liturgy supports, encourages, and reassures. Ritual remembrance in the Eucharist is essential to full Christian mystical prayer.

PRACTICE: Think of a way in which you can allow your participation in liturgical worship to nourish your private prayer.

Forgetting and Remembering

*T*o encounter God/Christ experientially, we must be able to forget ourselves except to the extent of being conscious of the experience of God/Christ's presence. To encounter God we must remember that God/Christ is alive, active, and communicating in this and every moment. Mystical prayer is diluted, dissipated, and clouded with darkness when our mind becomes engrossed with itself. When we remember an experience of God/Christ, we must beware of becoming fixed on remembering details rather than on the essential presence of God. However, remembering that God has been present can be a key to reestablishing the sense of God's presence in the present moment. Remembrance is far more powerful that we think. Let us not forget that for Christians it is the essential factor in the celebration of the Eucharist. Remember, then slip quickly into the awareness of the present moment with God.

Scripture and Sacramental Practice

Scripture is a constant in Christian prayer. It is a constant, living source. It would be difficult to overemphasize the dependence of mystical prayer upon scripture through the centuries. If mystical prayer is an effort to be conscious of the presence of God and if scripture is recognized as God's written word, the necessary connection is established.

For the non-Christian, the Hebrew scriptures or Old Testament remains a reservoir of incalculable riches, insight, knowledge, and wisdom. This is true also for the Christian. For the Christian the Hebrew scriptures represent God's promise of himself in writing, while the New Testament is the fulfillment of the promise. Hebrew scripture and history are rich in evidence of mystical encounters with God personified in such names as Abraham, Jacob, Moses, Isaiah, and David, and in such books as the Song of Songs and the Psalms. It can be fairly said that some of the most insightful early Christian mystical writings sprang from Old Testament scriptural encounters and commentaries, particularly those on the Song of Songs.

For the Christian, Christ is the focus of the mystical encounter with God. It cannot be repeated often enough that he is known from scripture with the Hebrew scriptures as root and promise and the Christian scriptures as the opening of the revelation into present and future, the beginning of fulfillment. Scripture also provides inspiration and expression in the living tradition and the external ritual so that liturgy is recognized as a vital expression and source of mystical life. The celebration of the liturgy with its dependence on scripture is often an affirming and strengthening of mystical experience. It is also a corrective to possible wanderings in private contemplative/mystical prayer.

Scriptural writings are not merely references to the past but are important and reassuring elements for a confident founding of our prayer in the here and now. The experience of scripturally inspired mystical prayer is not only through the insights of more modern scholars like Rahner but reflect a vibrant tradition of prayer reaching back to the beginnings of Christianity—and back again to the present moment.

We Must Remember

To truly pray, one must genuinely wish to communicate with God, be with God, and not just beg for some concrete favor. For the Christian this is always realized in and through Christ. It means that other voices must be stilled as much as possible to give precedence to an ever-awakening belief and sense of being in Christ's presence. This, in turn, requires periods of calm quietness and stillness. God is always giving; prayer is our receptiveness to that giving. We usually need to be calm and uncluttered to receive the gift even though God may occasionally surprise us.

We must also remember to have patience with our weakness and humanity. We are not yet accomplished saints. God is patient with us; so we must be patient with ourselves. Otherwise we will spend useless time thinking about ourselves instead of God in Christ.

Let us recapitulate here three of the potentially most common hindrances to growth in personal mystical prayer:

1. The assumption that mystical prayer is only for a select few, highly favored souls.
2. The impression that one must reach a certain high mark of proficiency before we can experience a sense of presence.
3. The times of darkness in prayer: Darkness is not the total loss of God/Christ awareness, but is a less immediate, compelling experience of presence. At such times we are not totally alone or lost, but living calmly by faith without the consolation of a sense of God's presence. Even the great mystics, almost without exception, report the sense of presence as coming and going, as brief and illusive.

Now Begin

Simply begin. This book is going to stop here. You may wish to return to and read the various individual segments as you need them. But establishing a sense of presence and becoming familiar with different uses of scripture is essential.

Setting a definite time and place for quiet and becoming familiar with presence is important for developing a truly full sense of prayer. Take courage. "The kingdom of God is *within* you!" Really!

All you need are:

A quiet time and place.
A mantra.
A Bible.

Recommended Reading

For anyone wishing to read the great mystics in their own words, the following books can be recommended:

Counsels of Light and Love of St. John of the Cross. Introduction by Thomas Merton. Mahwah, NJ: HiddenSpring, 2007.

Dupré, Louis, and James A. Wiseman, OSB, eds., *Light from Light: An Anthology of Christian Mysticism.* Second edition completely revised and updated. Mahwah, NJ: Paulist Press, 2001.

McGinn, Bernard, ed. *The Essential Writings of Christian Mysticism.* New York: Modern Library Classics, 2006.

Penrose, Mary E., *Refreshing Water from Ancient Wells: The Wisdom of Women Mystics.* Mahwah, NJ: Paulist Press, 2004.

ILLUMINATIONBOOKS

Other Books in the Series

Carrying the Cross with Christ
by Joseph T. Sullivan

Saintly Deacons
by Deacon Owen F. Cumming

Finding God Today
by E. Springs Steele

Hail Mary and Rhythmic Breathing
by Richard Galentino

The Eucharist
by Joseph M. Champlin

Gently Grieving
by Constance M. Mucha

Devotions for Caregivers
by Marilyn Driscoll

Be a Blessing
by Elizabeth M. Nagel

The Art of Affirmation
by Robert Furey

Jesus' Love Stories
by John F. Loya & Joseph A. Loya

Compassionate Awareness
by Adolfo Quezada

Finding a Grace-Filled Life
by Rick Mathis